S. Aggarwal

9 Ways to ~~Improve~~ Hate Yourself

Learn to Say No to Self-Improvement Principles that Instigate Feelings of Low Self-Worth. A Guide to Overcome Negativity and Self-Doubt

Acknowledgment

Writing "9 Ways to Hate Yourself" has been a journey of introspection and understanding, and I owe gratitude to those who have been instrumental in bringing this work to fruition.

First and foremost, I extend my heartfelt appreciation to my family for their unwavering support. Your encouragement and patience have been the pillars that sustained me through the challenges of this endeavor.

To my readers, thank you for embarking on this exploration with me. Your openness to diving into the complexities of self-discovery inspires and motivates me as an author.

I am indebted to all those individuals who shared their personal stories and experiences, contributing to the authenticity of this book. Your courage in opening up about the struggles of self-hatred has added a profound layer to these pages.

I thank all the authors and eminent personalities whose words I've quoted throughout my book. You have been my mentor on my entire journey. I've grown up reading your valuable texts, but I'm only adding my perspective to them this time. I want to acknowledge that my intention is never to hurt or criticize, but rather to illuminate the multifaceted nature of self-improvement.

Lastly, this book is a testament to your resilience to the countless voices that go unheard, those grappling with self-doubt and internal battles. May it serve as a source of solace and be your companion on your journey towards self-love.

Thank you all for being a part of this important conversation.

With gratitude,

Shruti Aggarwal

My Gift for You

As a token of appreciation for associating with me, I would like to offer you- **My free e-book, "Thoughts for Your Soul"**. This book is available to buy on Amazon, but I am offering it as my gift to you.

"Thoughts for Your Soul" is a self-reflection journal, coupled with guided meditations that invite you to explore your innermost thoughts, fostering personal growth and well-being. Ready to embark on this transformative adventure?

Scan the code below, share your email, and find your free copy waiting in your inbox. Your path to self-enlightenment begins now.

Table of Contents

Hating Yourself

Hatred is consuming. It swallows your peace of mind. It engulfs your happiness. It eats into your soul. You can never really exist in comfort if you incubate feelings of strong hate towards someone, especially if that someone is someone close to you, a family, or a friend.

Hatred is an immensely powerful and dominating feeling. It may often overpower our other feelings and become all-consuming. It has often been observed that the more we hate someone, the more we think about him/her, recall bitter experiences, curse them, blame them, and hate them even more. So, this process becomes a never-ending cycle and destroys our peace of mind.

But what happens when someone starts hating himself? What happens when our mind is at war with itself? What happens when the storm of this destructive feeling erupts within and is so violent that it blows away every trace of a person's existence?

Brace yourself for "9 ways to hate yourself." The pages of this book go beyond the surface. It's not just about facts; it's about feelings, the ones we often don't talk about.

Betty was the second child in a large family of five children. She grew up with teachers telling her that she was dull, and her parents telling her she was lazy. Betty's elder sister Casey was a bright student, and better looking. Being the eldest child, she got all the love and attention of their parents. All the other children that followed could not get the care they deserved, owing to their mother's never-ending chores, and their father's busy work schedule to cater to the needs of their large family.

Betty grew up in the shadow of her high-achieving sister and so she never felt adequate. She was good at a lot of things, like dancing and playing chess, but all her qualities often got overlooked. She was always seen as a lesser version of her sister. She always faced comparison and judgment.

She started to look down upon herself. By the time she could discover who she was, she had already known she was a worthless piece of sh*t. So, she shelled herself. She restrained herself from talking to or confronting people. She avoided social gatherings. She had no friends.

She felt a strange kind of loneliness, even when there were people around her. Her loneliness followed her everywhere, and it frightened her. She would sit for long hours feeling a weird emptiness and would not want to do anything. This started to reflect in her studies too. Her low grades would fetch her harsh comments from teachers, and ridicule from schoolmates. If this load of embarrassment and low self-worth was not enough, her parents' reaction to her report card would leave her in a deeper pit of self-doubt. She would see in their eyes loads of anger, then frustration, and then helplessness.

All this would leave her whirling in the tempest of self-hatred. She would loathe herself, curse herself, and blame herself. She had come to know for sure that she was the bad girl, so she started behaving like one. She started lying about small things. She would steal stuff from other's bags in school. She was burning inside with anger over the criticism and censure she had received all these years, while she craved approval. But outside she put on a stubborn face and would seem as if she was proud of what she was becoming.

Sometimes she would lock herself up in her room, curl up, and cry her heart out. She would look at herself in the mirror, scratch her face, and slap herself. She would stand at the window and think of jumping out. She had cut herself several times.

By the time she reached college, she was a drug addict, an acute alcoholic, and had slept with a dozen boys. Her parents were tired of scolding her, yelling at her, and locking her up in her room. They had concluded that she was the black sheep of the family and had left her to her fate.

Betty behaved in an extremely defensive way on the outside. But inside, she hated herself for doing the things she was doing. Her actions damaged her low self-esteem, even low, causing her to do even meaner deeds, creating a vicious circle.

Betty dropped out of college in her second year. Casey had married her long-time boyfriend by this time. Betty was still the same; In fact, she had developed even more bitterness for Casey. She hated her for being the "perfect child" of their family. She hated her for being the "perfect student" in school, and she hated her for the "perfect life" she was living now. One day Betty found Casey's husband alone at home and seduced him to bed. Casey caught them red-handed. This act made her fall in not only the eyes of all others but also her own eyes.

She was ashamed of herself. She had understood that she was the cause of all misery and that her existence was only a source of pain and shame to their family. She locked herself in her room. She looked at herself in the mirror but could not face herself. She curled up and cried. Then got up and went to the window and jumped out.

An innocent child, a beautiful creation of nature, was forced to live with low self-esteem. She was denied acceptance and appreciation. She was only looked at through the lens of perfection and thereby forced to live a perilous life. She was shunned, criticized, and judged to the extent that she started believing that she was inadequate, good for nothing, and worthless. She started hating herself.

It makes my heart cry to think how a child's different abilities or uniqueness lost the game to the grandeur of perfection. Why doing better or performing better, often becomes more important than living better? Why do a person's abilities need to be measured on a weighing scale to see if they conform to the set standards and thereby deserve to exist?

According to the World Health Organization (WHO), more deaths are caused by suicide every year than homicide or war. As per an estimation, roughly 85% of people worldwide including teens, adolescents, and adults, suffer from low self-esteem. Most of this lack of self-esteem emerges at an early age when children are either not listened to, when their accomplishments are not recognized, or they receive harsh criticism for their mistakes. Often children who experience the "perfect child" syndrome also end up with low self-esteem. Negative experiences in the social or academic environment, like bullying, harassment, or body shaming are the major contributors to lack of self-confidence in teens.

Once this low self-confidence sets in at an early age, it affects the child's perception of self, and the child starts to doubt his abilities and worth. The impressions of their past experiences are so engraved in their minds that they rarely emerge out of them. Instead, they find themselves falling into a deeper pit of self-denial and self-hatred. This seed of self-hatred once sprouted, spreads fast to entwine every aspect of the individual's identity, and branches endlessly into their future.

The Self-Improvement Trend

We live in a time where everyone wants more and wants to be more. Thanks to this age of ample opportunities and resources that can help us become who we aspire to be. Self-improvement, self-discipline, success, and productivity are the buzzwords today and people are spending a lot of their time and energy exploring ways to get better at work and life. So, everyone around wants to look better, feel healthier, earn higher, lead smarter, and become happier.

The self-improvement industry has grown manifold. The increasing demand for ideas, tips, tricks, strategies, and mantras that can catalyze this process of getting better, has given rise to more and more self-help books coming up, motivational speakers being born, self-improvement coaches and trainers emerging, and tons of YouTube videos popping up on social media. Each of these books, speakers, coaches, and trainers seems to know exactly what it needs to get better.

Just like you cook a bowl of instant noodles for yourself, in two minutes, people want instant success in their lives.

Everyone is looking for "you do it, and it's done" methods of making things better.

No doubt, a demand is always followed by a supply. The rising demand for guaranteed, instant, sure-shot success is causing a flood of coaching programs, seminars, motivational speeches, and books that boast of success in 30 days, 10 days, 7 days, or even less. All these programs talk about changing your mindset, aiming high, becoming the best version of yourself, awakening the giant within you, conquering your fears, and taking action.

People look up to coaches, mentors, and guides for every kind of problem that they face in life, whether it is scaling their business, deciding their career paths, doing better in their relationships, becoming better parents, improving their fitness, or developing spirituality. Instead of finding out for themselves, they want a ready-made solution to all that they yearn for in life.

The self-improvement process as prescribed by these experts seems amazingly simple and easy to achieve. It seems so luring that every individual starts feeling the need to improve in areas they never even thought they needed to get better at or work on. Such is the marketing strategy in today's world that creates within you the need for products and services you never thought you needed. You may relate to this when you go to departmental stores or supermarkets. Products are arranged so smartly on the shelves that you always end up buying much more stuff than you actually intended to.

Similarly, this growing trend of easy self-improvement is creating a growing need within people to improve in all areas of life. So, every person wants to become perfect in each and every aspect of their lives. He wants to have an extraordinarily successful career, perfect relationships, completely fit bodies, and a great lifestyle, and he also wants to parent his children well.

The Peril of Self-Improvement

The ongoing trend of self-improvement is forcing individuals to always keep trying to improve and get better. The growing unrest for a better life is forcing people to try everything off the shelf to find an answer to their unending quest.

While improving or getting better is a worthy endeavor, at least at the outset, it builds internal unrest in our minds. This unrest is about inefficiency and insufficiency and inability and inadequacy. This unrest is about a void or a lack that we always feel exists that never makes us feel complete or fulfilled.

It is not bad to improve. The entire history of human civilization is based on constant improvement and evolution to get better. From time immemorial we have been taught to direct our efforts towards getting better at what we are or what we do. But this current obsession with self-improvement, rising perfectionist tendencies, and the mad race for success and self-discipline is what draws my concern.

Pema Chodron, a great Buddhist speaker, talks about self-improvement as a form of self-aggression. She says that it makes you fall prey to an inner critic who says that you are not intrinsically whole or complete in the present moment. This inner critic says that "you're not enough" and we keep finding ways to fill that deficit. From trying to correct our imperfect bodies, to pushing ourselves to be more productive, to cursing ourselves to be messy, and to forcing ourselves to self-discipline; we constantly look for ways that can fill that deficit. The irony lies in the fact that this quest is never going to end, as that void can never be filled. Do you know why?

It is because there is actually no void. We are born complete and fulfilled but never realize that. We are frantically looking for something all around us. We don't even know what it is. We are trying to fill a glass that's already filled!

All those areas you feel you need to work on or improve, require us to connect with ourselves and create a conscious relationship with ourselves. So, what we require in place of self-criticism, self-improvement, and self-discipline is self-compassion, self-awareness, and self-consciousness with our soul. Instead of yearning for self-improvement, if we make self-acceptance and self-love the center of our endeavors, we can attain this fulfillment. By doing it in this positive and mindful fashion, we are able to fill that glass (or rather realize that it's full), rather than always seeing it as empty and making futile efforts to make it full.

What's wrong with filling the glass more?

So, what will happen if you try to fill a glass that's already full? It will spill. Your entire space will get messy. Isn't that what we are doing?

In trying to get better, we are criticizing, forcing, and torturing ourselves which is creating additional discontent. So, what looked messy or insufficient to you is becoming even messier. This unconscious form of self-aggression harms or completely damages your self-esteem. You get surrounded by a cloud of critical thoughts like, "I am not good," "I'm ugly", "I'm inefficient", and "I am not enough".

In its extreme form, self-improvement can go as far as becoming an obsession wherein you are constantly, disapproving of yourself, judging yourself, and comparing yourself to others. And this may result in self-loathing and self-hatred. This in turn can catapult into low self-esteem, depression, anxiety, and obsessive-compulsive disorders.

We need to come out of this self-improvement mindset and replace it with self-awareness and self-acceptance. The problem is that we have grown up with this belief that we need to constantly improve ourselves.

During our childhood, we were instructed to improve our manners and behaviors, improve in studies, compared to other children and our peers, were scolded for underperforming in academics, and were expected to be great in sports and other extra-curricular activities. As adults, we are expected to be better husbands, wives, parents, employees, or even better humans. On top of that, the additional pressure to improve that we pose on ourselves in trying to be better, look better, perform better, produce better, and live better has helped strengthen our embedded belief system.

We are always trying to be like someone else. We have set our standards as per which we do not approve of ourselves and thereby we are constantly trying to be what we are not. We are aiming for goals that are not ours. We are living by socially accepted norms rather than our own values.

The Problem with Self-Improvement

What would happen if you started whacking assess until they became horses? They would definitely one day become anything but horses.

I have the utmost problem with this concept of self-improvement. According to Einstein, "Everybody is a genius. But if you judge a fish by its ability to climb a tree, it will live its whole life believing that it is stupid." So, what I believe is that each one of us is gifted with abilities. Every human has a unique set of characteristics, thought patterns, behavior, and intelligence. We all are awesome at doing certain things, and at the same time, we may be awful at doing others.

The word improvement in itself implies making efforts to better something with respect to something that is an accepted standard. When we talk about self-improvement, we are only trying to compete with something or someone else or trying to measure up to them. This, according to me is the problem.

Firstly, who in the world has the right to define the standard units of a person's abilities or behaviors? There is no upper limit when it comes to a person's intelligence, potential, or capabilities. So, when you cannot measure these, how can you talk about improving upon them?

The second and the most crucial point is that none of us need improvement. If a person is looked upon as dull, unintelligent, or incapable of doing certain things, the problem is not with that person. The problem lies in the fact that we are unable to see, or rather we do not want to see the areas in which that person may be a genius. We are looking at one or two aspects of their character or behavior, and straight away passing the judgment that they need improvement.

This problem is so widely seen in every part of this society that it has become normal to look for improvement wherever a person seems to lack. Take for example our education system. In the prevailing education system, every child is loaded with the same language, mathematics, science, and humanities model, irrespective of their interests and abilities. Each child is expected to perform well in each of these subjects.

And it is so normal to see many of the students doing well in all of these subjects. But this according to me is a matter of training. When you train your brain to a certain extent, to do things even if they do not come naturally to you, you can do them to a certain level. It's like monkeys in a circus being trained to play drums. Even though monkeys are not meant to play drums, they do it in the circus, because they have been trained to do so. And to the amazement of the audience, a drummer monkey is born.

On the other hand, a few students who are unable to cope with one or two of the subjects given to them are straight away declared dull or unintelligent. The education system, their parents, their peers, everyone is of the unanimous opinion that they need to work hard, they need to improve.

Everyone, including the student himself, starts to believe that they need to improve themselves. Did anyone stop for a second, to think that maybe the child has some other interests? Maybe the child is an amazing painter or an artist. Or maybe the child has a great imaginative mind and can write amazing science-fiction stories. Or maybe he can become a wonderful cook because of his culinary skills.

We seldom look at these aspects. We simply judge and stamp them "Needs Improvement" on their heads and the poor child keeps banging that head against the walls in his quest for improvement throughout their lives. The present system is such that we have grown with this concept of trying to improve what we lack, instead of trying to find what we are great at. I am sure there are in each individual, several areas in which they may excel, but these areas are never discovered. Their unique talents often remain unexplored throughout their lives, and they keep wandering in their futile efforts of self-improvement.

This quest for improvement not only takes a person away from the real treasures they have within themselves but also lowers their self-worth, as they are always made to believe that they are less gifted than others. It creates limiting beliefs in their mind. They start feeling inadequate, and inefficient. And this is when self-improvement paves the way to self-doubt, low self-confidence, and self-hatred.

So, it is extremely important to create self-awareness to understand our true worth and abilities. Instead of trying to improve fish so that they could one day climb trees, we need to see their ability to swim beautifully in the water.

Instead of trying to mold and shape us to fit into the widely accepted standards, we need to discover our hidden gems. Being empathetic towards self and understanding ourselves is the correct way of living a fulfilling life.

The concept of self-improvement has a long time damaged the essence of humanity. It has always made us look at the world through a single lens and has deprived us of looking at the bigger picture which has many more colors to it, some of which still remain unidentified.

The world today is recognizing unseen and unexplored abilities in humans whom we once called disabled. We called them disabled because they could not do things ordinary people could do. But we are now realizing that these people are actually not disabled, they are different, and they are differently abled. When given an opportunity, some of these people have proved themselves by doing things ordinary people cannot. They have proved that they are beyond the ordinary and that they are extraordinary.

Stephen Wiltshire was born in London in 1974 and rapidly displayed many of the typical symptoms of ASD—he was nonverbal and appeared to live almost exclusively in his own world. He was diagnosed at the age of three and was unable to speak until the age of eight. But there was one thing he could do and do it amazingly well: sketch. He began sketching London's buildings, and the sketches were incredibly detailed—accurate down to the minute architectural detail, even after only a cursory scan. At the age of eight, he sold his first drawing, and the Prime Minister commissioned him to depict Salisbury Cathedral. Wiltshire's abilities were recognized as a Member of the Order of the British Empire by the time he was 32, and he got the esteemed opportunity to exhibit his work permanently at a gallery on the Royal Opera Arcade in London.

Jon Snow is one of the most accomplished television journalists in the United Kingdom, yet he struggled in school. He received a C in English but failed all of his other A-level subjects. He did not let his grades come in the path of his success. He believed in doing things that he loved to do. Snow attended college after high school to further his education, which led to admission to the University of Liverpool. In an interview, he advised pupils to focus on their abilities and to "want to do what you want to do very badly," adding, "There is life after A-levels."

Had these people focused only on their weaknesses and overlooked their special and unique abilities; they would have never achieved what they did. Had they only focused their endeavors on improving in the areas they lacked; they would have only lived a deficient life in which they would have always lived in coexistence with a void. They would have lived a life of insufficiency and inadequacy. This is what happens when we just try to keep improving ourselves. We end up in self-hatred.

Are Self-Improvement principles really improving life?

If Self-Improvement techniques could really make life better in any way, our world would have become a much happier place to live in. Keeping in view the increasing number of life coaching, self-development seminars, motivational summits, spiritual and wellness sessions, career counseling, and tons of self-help books on the shelves, the quality of human life should have become much better by now. More and more people all around the world would have been leading a fulfilled and blissful life. There would be increased mental satisfaction among people. Isn't it?

Well, the reports say just the opposite of this. According to a report by the World Health Organization in 2022, mental health issues have increased by 13% over the last decade. Around 20% of the world's children and adolescents have a mental health condition. WHO has also recognized self-guilt and low self-worth as the major symptoms among people struggling with depression.

Where do you think this self-guilt and low self-worth come from, if self-improvement principles were making your lives worthy and fulfilling?

This is the agony that lies behind this "better life" propaganda. This is the dark side of the self-improvement principles that prevail in the world today. More than the good that they do to a few, they hamper several others who are unable to keep pace, who fail to live up to societal standards, or who fail to achieve big dreams. There are millions who suffer from low self-esteem, and low self-confidence and end up hating themselves and their lives when they are left behind in their quest for a better life.

This book attempts to unleash the cons of some really hyped self-improvement principles, prevailing in our society. We have simply accepted these principles as cookie-cutters that decide and shape our lives stealing us of the liberty to live our life our way.

The coming 9 chapters are based on the 9 commonly advocated and widely accepted principles of self-improvement that come with a very dark side to it. Not only do these techniques of building self-discipline or achieving the so-called success, hamper one's peace of mind and cause unrest, but they also affect one's self-esteem in a way that they start hating themselves.

These are the "9 ways to ~~improve~~ hate yourself".

Chapter 1

The Paradox of an "Extraordinary Life"

"To live an extraordinary life, you must resist an ordinary approach."

– Frank McKinney

"Why live an ordinary life, when you can live an extraordinary one?"

– Tony Robbins

The entire world of self-help and personal development is spreading the pervasive message that urges everyone to strive for an extraordinary life. Self-improvement freaks are continuously talking about going above the average life, reaching out to greatness, and not settling for anything less than exceptional.

I don't intend to say that what is being said about achieving an extraordinary life is wrong. Nor do I challenge the intentions of its advocators. The problem lies in the way this concept is being interpreted by the world. The universe has now come to believe that success is all about pushing your limits, chasing grandiosity, and achieving big goals. While this concept may sound motivating and inspiring to success enthusiasts, it carries some potential drawbacks and grave consequences.

1. The incorrect interpretation of this concept
    Although there are no clear-cut boundaries to define what is "ordinary" and what's "extraordinary," an extraordinary life is often associated with greater material acquisitions, fame, or big achievements.
    So, a person who is doing a job, working **9-5**, or who makes enough to meet his family expenses, and also save a little, is an ordinary person. And an entrepreneur who has a multi-billion-dollar business, working **5-9**, and who hardly finds time to meet his family is extraordinary.
    What word are we trying to spread? Who has decided what the words average and above average mean? We cannot decide what is below average, average, or more than average only on the parameters of wealth or the so-called success. Are happiness and mental satisfaction nothing when deciding what level of life, a person is leading? How can anyone identify a person's level of life based on the bucks he earns? Maybe, a person loves the work he does but does not churn out millions out of it. Does that not qualify for an above-average or extraordinary life? What if someone is giving a limited time to work that's just enough to earn a decent income and loves to give

time to family, pursue a hobby, or engage in some social activity? Is it not a rewarding life? Not according to the modern standards of life, because the present industrial age measures everything in monitory standards. Success is equivalent to one's material acquisitions.

2. The pressure to be extraordinary.
    The idea of not settling for average or ordinary can create a tremendous amount of pressure and dissatisfaction. One may feel inadequate or unworthy if they do not measure up to these lofty societal

Ms. Simpson was a hardworking teacher who found joy and fulfillment in educating and empowering young minds. "I love the students and their continuing ability to amaze me. I thoroughly enjoy teaching and making a difference in children's lives. It is an honor to be in this role," she said. However, later in life she also started to feel that her profession was not considered cool like that of her other friends, some of whom were entrepreneurs, and media personnel.

Imagine how a person like Ms. Simpson may be faced with a paradoxical situation wherein she may feel that her job is not highly paid, or her profession is considered ordinary or average according to industry standards. She may feel inadequate. She may feel that she hasn't achieved extraordinary success.

She may start to develop doubts regarding something she actually loves doing. And instead of doing what she wants, she may be tempted to run behind the trends and the extraordinary, and thereby ruin her peace of mind. This constant pressure to be extraordinary can become a reason for her perpetual state of dissatisfaction and unrest. She may be tempted to do things that can never seek her fulfillment.

Therefore, in following this concept, instead of pursuing one's own dreams, one may always feel the unwanted pressure of doing things that society conceives as great, looking for more lucrative career opportunities, and achieving an extraordinary life.

3. The mindset of unrest

    The relentless pursuit of greatness and external validation can create a perpetual cycle of chasing happiness, always seeking the next milestone or achievement to fill a perceived void. This mindset often fails to acknowledge the importance of finding joy and fulfillment in the present moment and appreciating the ordinary aspects of life.

    People are unconsciously developing a mindset of constant struggle for perfection, and greatness. This constant striving for an extraordinary life can lead to a lack of satisfaction and contentment.

    This unrest mindset is becoming a widespread problem today. The people today are becoming increasingly impatient, unsatisfied, and restless. This unrest mindset is spreading like a virus and is especially targeting the younger generations. Have you noticed how our grandparents and our parents were quite calm, composed, and patient while our children are becoming increasingly anxious, irritable, and restless?

    Have you noticed that a few decades back, people continued in the same jobs for years, getting their yearly increments and promotions and leading a contended life? But today, there is a culture of switching jobs every now and then. People constantly switch jobs in search of new work environments, new experiences, better job profiles, and better salaries. It's not that they are totally wrong in doing so. But it shows the restlessness that has settled into the nerves of our younger generations. Also, there is no evident proof that this constant search for better opportunities is actually making their lives any better. Data shows that more people these days suffering from job and work stress.

The unrest mindset can also be seen in relationships these days. Impatience has so much affected the present generation that people fail to have steady and long-term relationships. The "break-up" and "patch-up" trend has become normal. People switch to new relationships as soon as something does not work, or there's something missing in their previous relationships. Relationships break at the slightest quarrel or misunderstanding as no one tries to give in time or effort to save them. They find it much easier to move on to a new partner. People have forgotten that good relationships do not depend upon finding a better partner, but on accepting and appreciating your partner for whatever he/she is.

This unrest is corroding our minds of our peace, contentment, and happiness. And instead of finding that happiness within us, we are frantically looking for it all around us.

The concept of extraordinary life has made people believe that they are meant for better things or rather the best things in life. The propaganda of this concept has caused people to keep looking for better and better in every area of their lives. This futile search for a better life makes them land nowhere. At the end of the day, they realize that they are running a mad race that has no end and that this race has only emptied them of their peace, patience, and stability.

4. Creating economic disparities
    The notion of pursuing an extraordinary life can also perpetuate economic disparities within society. Self-help teachings often imply that financial success and material possessions are markers of an extraordinary life. This focus on external measures of success can deepen the divide between those who have access to resources, opportunities, and privilege and those who do not. While it is important to aspire to improve our financial circumstances, defining an extraordinary life solely based on wealth and material possessions can be misleading. It disregards the inherent value and richness of a more balanced and fulfilled life that encompasses meaningful relationships, personal growth, and inner contentment.
    The concept of "extraordinary life" can cause some people to be looked down upon as ordinary and others to be looked up to as extraordinary. It creates demarcations within the society. The people so grouped as average or ordinary may end up with low self-esteem, and self-worth. On the other hand, they may also face unfair treatment from their so-called above-average counterparts.
    This concept of achieving an extraordinary life is a threat to our social structure.

Laura and Stacey were best friends in college. They were together all the time. In fact, when

Stacey got her first big modeling assignment, she chose Laura above her parents as the first person to share her joy with. Both girls were extremely happy and excited.

As Stacey started moving ahead in her modeling career, her ambitions kept soaring higher and higher. She kept striving for better opportunities and never cared about giving any time to friends or family. She considered it a waste of her precious time.

Even Laura after a certain stage started to feel the presence of a wide gap between them, as their lives were totally different now. Their lifestyles, their priorities, and their status were no match at all. She started feeling low about herself. She felt that she was an average person living a mediocre life. She started comparing every bit of her life with that of Stacey. She started judging her own life as inadequate. She doubted her abilities and worth and slowly began to hate herself and her life.

This concept of extraordinary life creates a rift so deep within our society that the so-called ordinary and the extraordinary fail to co-exist in harmony. It not only breaks our society but also breaks several loving relationships.

With all the above drawbacks I would rather call this concept a myth than a success principle. It's time we get over this myth and start looking at things from our own perspective and live a life based on our own values.

LET'S BREAK THIS MYTH!

The constant pursuit of an extraordinary life, as advocated by self-help gurus, can create undue pressure, economic disparities, and a lack of satisfaction. Instead of fixating on being extraordinary, it is crucial to embrace authenticity. It is essential to recognize that each person's journey is unique. Rather than solely focusing on extraordinary achievements, we should redefine success and fulfillment on our own terms. It is essential to acknowledge that greatness comes in various forms and may be different for each person. Success can be found in the everyday moments of life, in the love we give and receive, the impact we make on others' lives, and the personal growth we experience.

By shifting our perspective and embracing the beauty of ordinary moments, we can find greater satisfaction and contentment. It is about appreciating the journey, finding joy in the process of self-discovery, and living a life that is aligned with our true values and aspirations. Authenticity, self-acceptance, and embracing the ordinary aspects of life are powerful tools for finding fulfillment and creating a meaningful existence.

Now, let's replace this myth with affirmative statements that will help to create a new thought process. The old belief was deeply embedded in our system, so, it may definitely take some time to inculcate this new belief within us. But when we do it regularly with the help of positive, affirmative statements, we can reprogram our brains with this new belief.

SAY OUT LOUD:

- Whatever I love doing is my extraordinary way of life.

- Whatever gives me mental peace and satisfaction is my achievement.
- No one can decide my standards or my level of life.
- It's my life and I will only decide what's extra-ordinary for me.
- I don't need to force myself to do things I don't want to.
- I don't have to act in ways that don't align with my values.
- I don't care about what's great for others.
- I will only try to achieve greatness in things I care for, and I am already doing great.
- I am living an extraordinary life.

Chapter 2

The Illusion Of "Big Dreams"

"To achieve big things, you have to have big dreams."

– Conrad Hilton

"Believe big. The size of your success is determined by the size of your belief. Think little goals and expect little achievements."

– David J. Schwartz

Success is only about big dreams, big beliefs, and big achievements. The self-improvement industry has created a taboo in the minds of the people that achieving success only implies amassing immense wealth, achieving elevated levels of fame, attaining goals that almost seem impossible to others, or doing things that fetch you the world's awe and appreciation.

So, what do these advocators mean by "big dreams"?

Surely, they don't mean a student's dream to secure a good job after studies, a homemaker's dream to get a work-from-home job, or a freelancer's dream to get more projects.

The success-driven economy and its advocates have repeatedly talked about people who are highly successful. They have quoted examples of big entrepreneurs, leaders, sportspersons, or celebrities and established them as the standard icons of success.

 You ask a kid today to give some names of successful people, and he will straight away start with Bill Gates and end somewhere with Michael Phelps. Not to forget some other fancy names like Elon Musk, Steve Jobs, Donald Trump, Narendra Modi, Richard Branson, Oprah Winfrey, Mark Zuckerberg, Madonna, Stephen King, Beyonce, and Barack Obama. There's a very rare chance that the kid may say that perhaps my mom is a highly successful woman because she is the best at whatever she does. Gone are the days when children called their dads their superheroes because now, they are taught by the media that no one is a hero unless he is Elon Musk.

The other day, I saw my ten-year-old watching some silly video on my phone and asked him what it was. He raised his eyebrow and gave me a look, "You don't know who he is!" he said. "He is one of the most famous Youtubers in the world. Do you know how much he earns every day?"

This is the world we are living in today. Someone who earns high is considered the epitome of success and is idealized and worshipped by everyone. Success is only measured by any big achievements that you make (big as per the social standards).

During my high school days, I learned that work is said to be done when force is applied to a body and the body moves through a distance. That is how they described work in terms of Physics.

I grew up to understand, that doing work means producing goods and services that are of a certain value. That value may not always be monetary. Therefore, a doctor prescribing medicines to a patient is work and a priest giving a valuable sermon to a group of people is also doing work. This is because he is adding value to someone's life, even though he may/may not be paid for it. Similarly, a homemaker doing household chores is also doing work by rendering services that are important to the entire family, although she is not paid for it. (And often not accredited or appreciated for it).

But in the present success-driven world, work done is only and only equal to money earned. You can say you are doing great only when you are earning great.

So, what is the society advocating?

That everyone needs to become a Tim Cook, or an Oprah Winfrey, or Jeff Bezos. A great life is all about thinking big, achieving big, and living big. That people owning small businesses, working at small designations at corporate offices, or doing odd jobs to make a living are all unsuccessful people who deserve no applause or acclaim? That all workforces, manual laborers, or support staff are living a worthless life that they should be ashamed of?

The present-day society has created a taboo in the minds of the people that success is about owning a big company, wearing a business suit, being awarded at big events, being invited to management schools to give lectures on how they made it big, or making your country or the world proud of your achievements. That someone is proud of what he does, is of no relevance today. This means that unless you are an icon, an epitome of success, and a motivation to millions of other people, you are doing nothing you should be proud of.

Are we not trying to create more discomfort in the world? Are we not bringing human minds to unrest? Are we not adding to the dissatisfaction, discontent, and unhappiness in the world?

The world already is dealing with problems like stress, lack of job satisfaction, work pressures, etc. Instead of finding solutions that help people to feel internally satisfied and happy, we are creating additional stress and pressure by telling them that their dreams are small. We are continuously talking about dreaming big and aiming high. Imagine, how unmotivated a person might feel if told that what he/she is doing is nothing great or big. One can be totally shattered on the inside to learn that. This is what is actually happening in the world, hence the unrest.

This, "dream big" philosophy is making a massive impact in the minds of the people, especially on the youngsters. They want to achieve big success and they want to do it at any cost. They create larger-than-life dreams and resort to all sorts of methods to realize their dreams. They even do not refrain from following the wrong paths to make it big, because big is the trend.

You must have heard of the increasing cases of online scams, hacking, and cheating. Children drain away money playing online games in an effort to make quick and easy money from them. They adopt every "beg, borrow, or steal" method to make their big dreams come true.

My sister recently bought a new car, and the family went out for dinner to celebrate the moment. I was also a part of the small celebration. I saw my nephew (fourteen-year-old) sitting quietly in a corner and asked him why he wasn't joining us. To this, he replied, "We have not bought a Ferrari so that we celebrate. A small car like that is nothing one should be proud of." I was dumbfounded to hear what he said.

For several days I kept thinking, what made that little boy create that opinion? I then realized that it is this notion of "big goals, big dreams, and big achievements." That small car may be a big achievement for the family, but it doesn't seem big to him. Just because it is not so big that he can talk about it to his friends, he's kind of ashamed of it. For the younger generations today, happiness is only associated with expensive and luxurious stuff that they can show off or boast of in their friend or social circle.

Little joys of life, that give real happiness have lost their importance in the glitter and shine of bigger achievements most of which fail to give you any real contentment or happiness.

I don't say that one should not have big dreams, but they should be big in their own opinion, not in the opinion of others.

Therefore, this widespread principle of "having big dreams," is a myth than a success principle. True success lies in achieving objectives that you hold dear. They should be big for you, not for the world. We need to come out of this "dream-big" mindset as soon as possible before it corrodes the minds of the coming generations who would resort to every kind of ethical or unethical way to make their big dreams come true. That could be a real threat to our society.

LET'S BREAK THIS MYTH!

This dream big concept only creates insufficiency and inadequacy. One should create dreams that are in alignment with their own values, preferences, and beliefs. So, if your passion is writing, do not bother if your dream of authoring great books seems big to others or not. Pursue your dreams because only they can give you the ultimate sense of fulfillment and accomplishment.

The quest of following big dreams according to societal standards can deviate you from your real goals. Such dreams will never be a source of joy, even if you achieve them.

Identify what success means to you and then decide your ideals. Your success icon can be your friend who secured low grades initially but worked hard to improve his grades. You can also idealize your gym-mate who was very irregular but has now created a religious routine of attending the gym. Your epitome of success need not be the world's richest, strongest, or fastest, or the most famous person. He only must be someone who inspires you and helps you become a better version of yourself.

Big and small are very relative terms. What seems big to you may be small for the other, and inconspicuous to yet another person. Identify what's big for you. **Remember, that "your big" is the only "big" that really matters to you.**

Now, let us bust this myth with the help of positive affirmations. These affirmations will help you build trust in your own dreams and will help to create self-worth and confidence. When you have faith in your dreams, you will gain fulfillment and happiness in achieving them.

SAY OUT LOUD:

- I am a successful person.
- I have my own dreams in life.
- My dreams are particularly important to me.
- They are the driving force for my actions.
- My dreams motivate me.
- I aim to achieve my dreams very soon.
- I love the journey I am headed on.
- I enjoy every moment of it.
- I celebrate my little achievements.
- My achievements give me joy and fulfillment.
- My achievements are big for me.
- Therefore, I am a successful person.

Chapter 3

The Fallacy Of "Deriving Inspiration from Others"

"The best way to be successful is to learn from other successful people."

– Martin Dai Nguyen

"Surround yourself with positive, energetic, successful people and learn from them."

– Robert Cheeke

Most self-improvement books talk about looking up to people who have done great in their field and trying to learn from their journey and their mistakes. They advise you to take inspiration from their life and walk in their footsteps to fast-track your success journey.

While the self-help gurus would advise taking motivation or inspiration from others who have done considerably well, learning from their mistakes, and following the path that they took, the truth about deriving motivation from others is that it can often be bad than good. When we try to look into the lives of others, who according to us have achieved much, we often end up judging ourselves for not being efficient, disciplined, will-powered, or lucky like them. We create additional inadequacy in our minds by comparing our lives to theirs and end up in frustration and self-hatred. When these techniques of building self-discipline do not work and we give up after a few days of trying, we end up blaming ourselves, our family, our circumstances, our fate, or even our creator.

The luring lives of people as they appear on social media are rather fake than real. Their happiness and fulfillment are in reality far behind what appears in their Facebook and Instagram posts. Their lives are not actually that healthy, and their careers that flourishing, and their relationship that sorted. Behind the healthy lifestyle that they show to the world is their obsessive race of looking fit and healthy for which they have to bear the brunt of self-aggression. Behind those high-income statements, one fails to see the burdens of debt and mental pressures, and behind those warm couple photos, lies the agony of mistrust, lack of time, communication, and true love.

But the world takes what they see to be the ultimate truth. So, when they look at others they get seduced by their success, their life, and their relationships. Their inner perfectionist is awakened, and they want to be as good, as slim, as healthy, as successful, and as happy as them. Instead of deriving motivation, they start comparing themselves and their lives to them. We want to achieve that same level as we take them to be the standard units for measuring our progress. So, our goals are generally not our own goals, they are the goals that we create with respect or under the influence of the people who we consider to be our ideals.

In the self-help industry they commonly say that if you follow the path laid down by the great, you will get success. So, everyone wants the success pill; the no effort, no tension, no failure pill that guarantees you sheer success. Even though it is not as easy as it may sound, even if you happen to find success by following others, do think it will be a source of fulfillment?

Actually no! Have you heard of some extraordinarily rich and effective people who are extremely unsatisfied within? Heads of several multinational companies who gave up everything to become monks? Or some celebrities who may have a high-profile life but actually live on pills to combat their anxiety or depression? And artists who end up taking drugs to suppress their inner conflicts? When you follow the success path laid down by others, you are being driven by the results they achieved from it. You are being driven by the end and not the journey. You are aiming for goals that you don't even know are actually yours. Such goals, even if they may bring you volumes of wealth or fame, may be insufficient to satiate your inner desire for fulfillment.

The reality is that, if you don't love what you do, you will not do it long. So, when you are embracing a career or walking up a path only because some others who walked the same path became successful, you are shutting down the doors on self-realization. You are listening to the world that talks about shortcuts to success or happiness but you are unhearing the voice within. "Don't follow the path. Blaze the trail" says Jordan Belfort.

When you follow dreams that are yours, when you create your own path and mindfully accept the successes and failures that come along, your journey becomes an adventurous trail and you will love to walk it, after all, who doesn't love adventure? When you do that, you won't require any external factors to motivate you. Your journey itself would be a strong motivational force to get you going, every single day.

Let's take an example: Most of us need to push ourselves to get to work each day. We hate our jobs. Imagine every day you had to get up to go on an adventurous trip, exploring new territories, and gaining new experiences. Would we not be thrilled and excited to go each day? Would we not charge out of our bed every day to see what's coming today?

This is just an example. What needs to be understood is that, when we are doing things that we really love doing, we have motivation enough and a strong driving force that keeps us charged.

A friend of mine has a passion for baking. She started her career in baking when friends and family started giving her orders because her cakes were delicious. Then she took it seriously. It's been fifteen years now and she gets orders of all kinds of weird and sometimes enormous sizes of cakes. Every order is a new challenge for her and I see her excitement whenever she gets a new order. "I keep imagining while in bed, what I would be doing differently this time, and can't wait to start working on it the next morning," she says. It's not that she owns a multi-million business; she just loves doing what she does.

The problem is that most of us, believe me, most of us are not doing what we love to do. We are either doing what other successful people do, what looks rewarding, what is in trend, or what has been established as a standard in our society. So, if you want to lose weight it's not because you feel the need for a healthy and fit body, it's mostly because all other women in your social circle have lean figures. And that's the reason you have no internal motivation or drive for it. You force yourself, push yourself, and beat yourself to achieve that goal, but soon give up. You look at others for motivation, but instead end up with frustration, self-loathing, and self-hatred.

The truth about deriving motivation from other successful people is that it does more bad than good. Firstly, we look only at their success. We totally ignore the pressure they experience, the stress they live with, and the torture they inflict upon themselves to achieve that success.

The second reason is, that the lives displayed by the people we admire are often misleading. There is often a dark reality behind it. The people whose footsteps we want to follow, those whose lives appear to be highly sorted and fulfilling, are often faking their lives. Often they create a virtual life that looks so perfect on the outside but is not so perfect, sometimes crippled inside. We see the fresh and beautiful side of an apple whose rotten side is hidden.

Third, when we follow the success trail set by others, we forget our own values and align our goals with theirs. This leads to an internal void because at the end of the day, even if you achieve success, you realize you never yearned for it because the goals you achieved were not yours. They were the dreams borrowed from someone else.

Lastly, deriving motivation from others often ends up in comparison, self-judgment, self-criticism, and hatred.

LET'S BREAK THIS MYTH!

True fulfillment in life comes not from merely mimicking the paths of other successful individuals, but from forging a unique journey guided by one's own aspirations and values. While emulating the achievements of others may offer short-term gains, genuine contentment is derived from pursuing personal goals that resonate with the core essence of one's being.

Each individual possesses a distinct set of passions, beliefs, and dreams, which serve as the compass to a purpose-driven life. By charting a course that aligns with these inner values, one taps into an authentic wellspring of motivation and resilience, propelling them toward fulfillment. Embracing this self-directed approach empowers individuals to cultivate their own talents, learn from their own experiences, and create a legacy that is a true reflection of their uniqueness.

While mirroring others will lead to jealousy, comparison, and frustration, it can cause a person to feel inefficient, inadequate, and incapable. It can kill a person's self-worth and lead to self-hatred.

Let's come out of this mindset and create a fresh mindset with the help of positive affirmations.

SAY OUT LOUD:

- I have my own goals in life.
- I align my life goals on the basis of my own values.
- I do not need to compare myself to others.
- I do not need to do things others are doing.

- I do not need to be harsh on myself for acting in accordance with others.
- I do not need to judge myself on the basis of the progress of others.
- I do not rely on others for motivation.
- I love what I do.
- I love my journey and not just the result of it.
- My journey is my motivation in life.
- I am aware of my values, and my limitations.
- I celebrate the uniqueness that sets me apart and fuels my success.
- I can progress on my journey with self-acceptance.
- My life's fulfillment is the result of my authentic pursuit of my passions and values.

If you have been reading self-help books for a long time and have tried a few of the ideas that they advocate, you are awesome. If you have been able to keep up the good habits and have achieved some form of self-improvement, congratulations! I wish more power to you.

I am not against the self-improvement industry. I would not say that nothing they preach, actually works; but I would definitely say that there is a dark side to it. A person may or may not derive benefit from it, but he/she definitely is affected by this darker side of it. In the next chapter, we will discuss one of the most important self-improvement advice that according to self-help gurus guarantees success, "time management".

Chapter 4

The Trap of "Time Management"

"Either you run the day, or the day runs you."

- Jim Rohn

"The key to time management is to see value in every moment."

- Menachem Mendel Schneerson

Time management has become a buzzword in the self-improvement industry, promising increased productivity, reduced stress, and a sense of control over our lives. We are bombarded with various techniques and strategies, each claiming to be the ultimate solution to managing our time effectively. From waking up early to meticulously planning every minute of our day, these techniques are hailed as the keys to success and fulfillment. However, the relentless pursuit of efficiency often leads to heightened stress, anxiety, and a nagging sense of unrest.

Let's delve into some of the most commonly advocated time-management techniques and explore their unintended consequences.

1. The early bird gets the worm.

One prevalent technique endorsed by self-help gurus is the practice of waking up early. The self-improvement industry quotes the habits of successful people, and one thing that comes up, over and over is: Successful people tend to wake up early. The idea behind this technique is that by starting our day before the rest of the world, we gain a head start and maximize productivity.

While there are indeed benefits to aligning our routines with the natural rhythms of the day, it may not work for everyone. Our bodies and minds have unique rhythms, and forcing an early wake-up time might disrupt the delicate balance of our natural sleep patterns. Dr. Michael Breus in his book, "The Power of When," helps readers figure out their biological predisposition to be a morning person, evening person, or somewhere in between, and then figure out their ideal daily routine based on that predisposition. Breus is a clinical psychologist and sleep expert. Research led Breus to come up with four chronotypes - or four types of preferences for 'morningness' and 'eveningness'.

Therefore this "one size fits all" concept may not be rewarding for everyone. A person who is naturally not a morning person may feel highly pressurized to follow a morning schedule and it may affect his/her productivity and performance negatively. Moreover, the person may feel unnecessary stress. It can also lead to chronic sleep deprivation and a compromised immune system. Therefore, one must understand his sleep schedules and requirements carefully before blindly following this much-hyped concept.

Another important reason why this "early rising" concept may not work is that the world today is adopting a "late-night culture". Early-to-bed and early-to-rise days are gone. Often people, who wake up early, do not get to bed early. Demanding work commitments, social engagements, and the allure of 24/7 digital connectivity often extend well into the evening hours, making it challenging to unwind and retire early. Lifestyle, work schedules, and culture force people to stay up late and then face the day early. As a result, attempting to adhere to an early morning routine amidst these modern lifestyle demands can exacerbate stress and sleep deprivation. This lack of sleep may lead to several health problems, some of which may be chronic.

When self-help experts declare that in order to become successful, you need to wake up early or give examples of CEOs of big companies who are all early risers, it creates pressure on everybody else. One starts to feel that he/she can never become successful unless they conform to this "early riser" ideal. This can lead to anxiety and a sense of inadequacy in those whose bodies operate on a different schedule.

If I talk about myself, I am in no way a morning person. Getting up early to attend work and chores sounds torturous to me. It makes me feel deprived, anxious and stressed. An early morning alarm almost sounds like death to me. But that doesn't mean I do not complete the tasks I have set for the day. Most of my creative work finds accomplishment during the evenings, and that's the time I get maximum productivity.

You have heard about famous personalities who rise quite early, but I'm sure there must be many of those who may not be rising early but may still be successful. One needs to find his own sleep and work schedules that enable productivity but are not harsh or torturous to their physical and mental health.

2.   Following a fixed schedule

Another time-management technique propagated by self-help gurus is the idea of adhering to a fixed schedule. Self-improvement advocates argue that by allocating specific time slots for different activities, we can make the most of our day and ensure optimal productivity.

People, who live by self-improvement advice, diligently follow a fixed schedule, meticulously assigning time slots to various work-related tasks, personal pursuits, and leisure activities. While initially, they may feel a sense of control and order, they soon realize that life does not always adhere to a predetermined schedule. Unexpected demands, interruptions, and unforeseen circumstances frequently disrupt their well-planned agenda. Instead of adapting and embracing the ebb and flow of life, they feel frustrated and defeated when their schedule is thrown off course. The very structure that was meant to bring efficiency and harmony becomes a source of stress and inflexibility.

Often when people follow a dedicated schedule and are faced with some unforeseen task demanding their time, their personal time or family time gets compromised. They put in extra hours to their work and as a result, end up spending less and less time with friends and family. This results in unhappy and unsatisfied relationships. And as I always say, "Relationships are the basis of our lives." Unhappiness in relationships very soon becomes all-consuming and the person is bound to feel unhappy and unsatisfied in all areas of life. Sticking to schedules may/or may not make you successful but will surely give you frustration, irritable behavior, and an unhappy life.

Often when people prioritize work in their daily schedules, which they always do, they lose touch with close friends and relatives. They are often called arrogant for refusing get-togethers and outings.

When people stick to a fixed schedule, they also end up giving less time to leisure activities. This is because although they have allocated a specific time for them, they are the ones compromised every time there is an emergency. This may be harmful to their brain as it does not get the much-required break. This can give rise to stress and frustration. Life becomes machine-like and deprived of all emotions.

The rigid nature of a fixed schedule can create a sense of confinement and unrealistic expectations. It can lead to mental fatigue and tiredness. One may feel trapped in the vicious routine and start to hate their life.

Life is inherently dynamic and unpredictable, and attempting to fit every moment into a predefined timetable can rob individuals of the flexibility needed to adapt and enjoy life's spontaneity.

3. Multitasking

In the pursuit of efficiency, multitasking is often hailed as a valuable skill to master. The ability to juggle multiple tasks simultaneously seems appealing, promising increased productivity and time savings. However, the reality is that multitasking often leads to decreased focus, heightened stress, and a diminished sense of accomplishment.

Attempting to do more than one task at a time in order to complete more work in less time, often seems effective, but is actually counterproductive. This is because our brain is designed to perform one task at a time unless we have special training.

Focusing on a single task is a better approach than trying to do multiple things at a time. It helps your mind have clarity of goals which then actively creates ideas and issues instructions with a single goal in view and the result is that you get more work done, more efficiently. Moreover, focusing on a particular task and working on it continuously makes you enter the "flow zone." When you work in a state of flow, you give room for more creativity and insight. Multitasking, on the other hand, hinders creativity by not letting you focus on any one task at a time.

The unintended consequences of these time-management techniques are far-reaching. The never-ending pursuit of efficiency and the pressure to optimize every minute of our day often leads to heightened stress, anxiety, and a persistent feeling of unrest. We find ourselves constantly striving to meet unrealistic expectations, berating ourselves for any perceived time wasted or deviation from the plan. The pursuit of productivity becomes an ongoing race, leaving little room for spontaneity, creativity, and genuine enjoyment of life's simple pleasures.

LET'S BUST THE MYTH!

As we navigate the world of time management, it is essential to remember that true well-being cannot be measured solely by productivity or efficiency. Finding a healthy balance that allows for flexibility, self-compassion, and meaningful connections is crucial in our journey toward a more fulfilling and sustainable life.

Living a life of fulfillment and self-acceptance and escaping the time management trap requires a shift in mindset and adopting certain practices.

Take time to understand what truly matters to you and align your daily activities with your core values. This reflection will help you identify what brings you joy, fulfillment, and a sense of purpose.

It is crucial to prioritize individual well-being over societal expectations, allowing people to find their own rhythms for optimal productivity and sustainable health.

Understand that your worth is not solely defined by your professional achievements or the number of tasks you complete. Dedicate time to nurture relationships, engage in hobbies, and take care of your physical and mental well-being. Balancing your personal and professional life is essential for overall satisfaction and avoiding burnout.

Positive affirmations can be powerful tools for developing a relaxed mindset. Here are a few affirmations to incorporate into your daily life:

SAY OUT LOUD:

- I am deserving of happiness, fulfillment, and peace.
- I release the need to control time and embrace the present moment.

- I prioritize my well-being and create a balanced and fulfilling life.
- I trust in the natural flow of life and allow things to unfold at their own pace.
- I am enough, and my worth is not determined by how much I accomplish.
- I choose to live in the present moment and savor each experience.
- I let go of the need to rush and trust that everything will be accomplished in divine timing.

Remember, the journey towards a fulfilling and relaxed life is a continuous process. Embrace self-acceptance, practice patience, and be gentle with yourself as you navigate this transformative path.

Chapter 5

The Mad Quest of "Productivity"

"Productivity is the deliberate, strategic investment of your time, talent, intelligence, energy, resources, and opportunities in a manner calculated to move you measurably closer to meaningful goals."

- Dan S. Kennedy

"Productivity isn't about being a workhorse. Keeping busy or burning the midnight oil... It's more about priorities, planning, and fiercely protecting your time."

- Gary Keller

These amazing quotes are sure to fuel the productivity drives of the most ambitious people around. But to me, they sound like a program designed to produce productivity maniacs or robots that lack any human emotion. Andrew Wilkinson, founder of Meta Lab says, "Most successful people are just a walking anxiety disorder harnessed for productivity." Often productivity advice is only about carefully planning, strategizing, and 'fiercely protecting' every minute of your life. None of them talk about living every moment of your life.

During the past decade, the pursuit of productivity has become a cultural obsession. "Productivity" is the mantra chanted every day in corporate corridors, educational set-ups, and motivational or self-improvement organizations. The productivity-obsessed society has created a mad race wherein you are expected to be productive throughout your day, utilize every second to its maximum, push your limits, and constantly strive to outdo yourself and others.

From the moment you wake up, you are expected to be constantly productive, doing things that add value, without wasting a minute. We are told that success and fulfillment can only be achieved when we remain productive throughout our day and strive to increase our productivity with every passing day.

The modern world, with its rapid pace, has embraced productivity as its ultimate muse. This word has now woven itself into the fabric of our lives. We are now measuring our life's worth in terms of how productive we are. From boardrooms to classrooms, it's the numeric data of productivity that only matters.

But, in a world where "doing more," is celebrated, the simple art of "being," is getting overshadowed. There is no time for self-awareness or self-reflection. A person who runs the productivity race is often not clear about his whys in life. He does not know what he really wants in life. He is simply following the herd of productivity enthusiasts, who boast of having a great life. Therefore, even a highly productive and successful life cannot grant him internal peace and satisfaction.

The self-improvement experts are creating a belief that if we are not constantly busy and productive; we are somehow failing at life. The whack-your-ass lifestyle as advocated by the productivity gurus is exhausting. This obsession not only exhausts people during the day, but it also doesn't let the mind shut down at night. This overload tends to deplete their mind and body and becomes a cause of increasing stress, anxiety, and desperation.

The constant pressure to do more, achieve more, and be more leaves us feeling overwhelmed. We find ourselves trapped in a never-ending cycle of aspiring, achieving, and improving. And in this quest, we forget to live life. We accept life as a race, in which each of us keeps striving to come first. We keep running, ignoring the beautiful moments of life. We fail to enjoy the beauties of nature, the changing seasons, the beautiful days, and the starry nights. Life becomes more of a competition, than a journey of different experiences, good and bad. We forget to laugh at our silly acts, learn from our mistakes, and take lessons from what life teaches us.

The pressure to be more productive seeps into every aspect of our lives, from work to personal relationships, leaving little room for rest and relaxation. We forget that our mind and body need rest. We treat them like machines counting their per-hour production and completely ignoring the fact that even machines need rest. Scheduling, managing time, and multitasking all the time destroy our peace of mind. This obsession with productivity soon starts to take a toll on our mental health. It leaves us feeling overwhelmed, stressed, and anxious.

The productivity quest often leads to self-torture in the form of self-criticism and self-judgment. We berate ourselves for any perceived lack of productivity, believing that our worth is tied solely to our achievements. This constant self-criticism erodes our self-esteem and creates a deep sense of inadequacy.

Moreover, the mad race for productivity leaves little room for self-care and work-life balance. We simply ignore vital lifestyle requirements like meditation and exercise. Our busy work schedules often do not allow the luxury of a dedicated health and fitness regime. We sacrifice our physical and mental well-being in the pursuit of increased output. Long working hours, neglecting personal relationships, and constant stress take a toll on our health and overall quality of life. We become trapped in a vicious cycle where our worth is determined by our productivity, and any moment of rest or relaxation is seen as a failure.

"You will never feel truly satisfied by work until you are satisfied by life." –Heather Schuck, (The Working Mom Manifesto). The mad race of productivity often affects our relationships adversely. We tend to ignore our relationships. We fail to give adequate time and attention to our friends, families, and loved ones due to which our relationships suffer. People often fail to find time to connect with their loved ones, spend time with their children, and play with their pets, owing to their hectic work schedules. You must have often heard children of phenomenally successful and productive parents complain of a neglected and unloved childhood. Partners, who often crave love, time, and attention from each other, end up in divorce. Parents starve for the tiniest conversation with their children when the latter are busy and do not see them for days.

It is important to note that relationships form the basis of our lives. An extraordinarily successful life is worthless if you have none to share the joy of it. Strained relationships can never let you live in peace with your inner self. You may look happy with your success on the outside, but it is the love and care of someone that can give you your true smile. If you want to know more about creating strong relationships, that last a lifetime, you can read my book, "The Perfect Book for Imperfect Couples." This book can be your ultimate guide in creating that beautiful relationship you long for.

We need to understand that our worth is not determined by the number of things on our to-do list. Productivity is not just about doing things that are of monetary or material importance. It is important to make time for ourselves, make time for things, and people who matter to us –after all, it's our life. The mad quest for productivity often gets very superficial and shallow.

IT'S TIME WE BREAK THIS MYTH!

The race for productivity as interpreted by most people often is about producing increased goods, services, ideas, projects, and presentations, reading and responding to emails, getting more work done from employees, putting in more hours of work, and so on. Did you ever think that going around shopping with friends, enjoying a date with your spouse, having a relaxed dinner time with family, just sitting by yourself with a cup of coffee, or watching your favorite web series can also be called being productive?

We are human. We need much more than money, material possessions, work recognition, and entrepreneurial success.

We need love. We need respect. We need relationships. We need peace of mind. We need moments of self-reflection. We need clarity of purpose. We need self-empathy and understanding.

Therefore, it is important to understand that when we take a break from work, we are building our mental health. When we chat around with co-workers, we are building strong work relations. When we go for lunch with our spouse, we are building love in our personal relations. When we plan a holiday with family, we build beautiful memories we will cherish for life.

All these moments when we thought we were being unproductive; all this time we thought we had wasted, we were actually being productive. We were building beautiful relationships. We were creating bonds that would not only become the basis of our true happiness in life but would also become our strength in times when we feel weak.

Productivity does not only imply building a material-rich life, but it also implies building an emotionally and mentally rich life. It implies listening to our heart, and our mind. It implies understanding our emotions and feelings.

It's harsh the way this concept of productivity has swept away the intricacy of human feelings and emotions under the rug. We are told to simply unhear our minds because they say, "Our minds are pleasure-seeking," "Our minds are fearful of taking action," and so on.

People who unhear their inner calls, although may become extremely successful for the world, they lack inside.

Tom Shadyac, a famous Hollywood filmmaker lived a rich lifestyle until he realized he wasn't happy inside.

In an interview with Oprah, he revealed that he felt an emptiness, a void despite having almost everything money could buy. It is then he discovered that living within your means and sharing all the surplus you possess with the less fortunate is the way to live a truly happy life.

He gave away all that he owned to embrace a simple way of life. He said he felt happier and wealthier than ever before.

The truest measure of progress lies not only in the buildings we raise or the profits we amass, but in the smiles we share, the tears we wipe away, the bonds we build, and in the mindful moments of quiet reflection and self-understanding, that help us derive the true meaning of our existence.

Let us look at productivity as a more holistic concept with the help of powerful affirmations.

SAY OUT LOUD:

1. "I prioritize my well-being over constant productivity, understanding that my mental health is essential for overall success."
2. "My value is not solely determined by my productivity, and I embrace the importance of balance in my life."
3. "I release the pressure to always be productive, allowing myself moments of rest and relaxation without guilt."
4. "My self-worth is not tied to my accomplishments; I am enough just as I am."

5. "I cultivate a positive relationship with time, understanding that it is okay to progress at a pace that aligns with my well-being."

6. "I choose to measure success by my overall happiness and fulfillment rather than by external markers of productivity."

7. "I release the need for constant busyness and trust that moments of stillness contribute to my mental clarity and creativity."

8. "I honor my emotions and give myself space to feel, acknowledging that productivity does not require the suppression of my feelings."

9. "I am kind to myself in moments of perceived 'non-productivity,' understanding that breaks and downtime are essential for my overall productivity and happiness."

10. "I release the need to always strive for productivity at the expense of personal or family time, understanding that a balanced life includes moments of joy and connection."

11. "I prioritize quality time with my loved ones, understanding that the richness of my relationships holds more significance than the quantity of tasks accomplished."

12. "I embrace a holistic view of success that encompasses mental, emotional, and physical health, recognizing their interconnectedness."

Chapter 6

The Illusion of "Willpower"

"Willpower is the key to success. Successful people strive no matter what they feel by applying their will to overcome apathy, doubt, or fear."

- Dan Millman

"People with a strong willpower will always have the bigger picture in mind. They will be able to forgo small pleasures in order to help attain bigger goals.

- Brian Adams

Willpower is often apprised of as the key to achieving life goals. It is said that when we learn to break bad habits, cultivate good ones, and stick to them, we cultivate self-discipline, and this can be done only with strong willpower.

We are led to believe that if only we had more willpower, we could conquer any challenge and transform our lives.

How beautifully the above-quoted great men say, 'no matter what they feel,' and 'forego small pleasures' to attain success in life. They simply ignore the fact that we are humans. We are driven by feelings, emotions, and desires. Neglecting and unhearing our minds will only take us away from self-reflection and understanding.

For me, the joy of playing and binging on an ice cream with my son is more rewarding than sharing with him the happiness of my 'best employee' reward. When we only keep the bigger picture in mind, we miss the little moments of joy that actually leave more lasting memories to cherish for life.

Almost every self-discipline book and article talks about the famous "Marshmallow test", about research conducted in 1972 at the University of Stanford by Psychologist Walter Mischel. If you aren't aware of it, let me summarize it for you.

In this research, a group of children were given marshmallows each and left in a room unattended. They were instructed that if they do not eat it now, and wait till the instructor is back, they will be rewarded with a second marshmallow.

The results were as most of you would predict. Some of them ate their marshmallows instantly paying their marshmallows the much-needed respect by providing them their most deserving place (their tummy). Some others like me, the fickle-headed ones, tossed in their seats for a while, but finally stuffed it into their mouths, and down their throat without another thought. Well, the most disciplined ones, to the envy of all others, could hold on to their temptations and thus win their second treat.

And as the research continued, all these children were tracked as they grew up and later it was concluded that the children who had shown greater self-discipline and avoided instant gratification, were found to be better leaders, better decision-makers, and performed better in their life and careers.

So, that was all about the famous marshmallow test. Now, every self-help author, coach, speaker, and writer literally swears by delayed gratification as a recipe for success. Take for instance James Clear of Atomic Habits, who says, "Success usually comes down to choosing the pain of discipline over the ease of distraction. And that's exactly what delayed gratification is all about".

In the pursuit of success, we are often advised to embrace pain in the form of delayed gratification. The idea is that by resisting immediate temptations and sacrificing short-term pleasures, we can achieve long-term goals and reap greater rewards in the future.

But this rewarding future comes at a price. And the price is to deprive yourself of everything that seems great, tastes great, sounds great, and feels great. Deprive yourself of everything you love. You must burn your present in the agony of deprivation to lighten your unforeseen future, and that's never easy to do.

Building self-discipline means challenging your willpower. It means saying "no" to things you love. Pleasures are considered a sin, and a pleasure-seeking person is a sinner. He is often considered weak-willed, lazy, or unambitious. People look down upon him as he doesn't fit in the prevailing molds of perfection.

While there is merit in developing discipline and patience, the emphasis on delayed gratification can be extremely harsh on a person's self-esteem. This chapter delves into the pitfalls of this mindset and explores the detrimental effects it can have on one's sense of worth and emotional well-being.

The idea of willpower is deeply ingrained in our culture. We are constantly bombarded with messages telling us to "just do it" and "push through pain." We are made to believe that if we can't resist temptations or stay motivated, it's a sign of weakness. This societal pressure to display unwavering willpower can have detrimental effects on our mental and emotional well-being.

In this society that glorifies self-discipline and delayed gratification, individuals who struggle to resist temptations are often labeled as unworthy or undeserving of success. The belief that one's ability to delay gratification directly correlates with their worthiness as a person, can lead to a damaging cycle of self-judgment and low self-esteem.

When a person is unable to resist temptations despite trying repeatedly, he ends up in self-loathing and criticism. He shuns himself and ends up believing that he is unlike others. He creates negative self-belief that maybe he is not born with similar abilities and strength alike others. This creates within him inadequacy and low self-worth. This situation can destroy the person on the inside.

It is human nature to get intrigued to do things you are told not to. So, if I say, "Don't look back," most of you are bound to look back almost instantly. Similarly, when you are trying to resist temptations, you get drawn towards them. You think about them, fancy them, avoid them, and end up thinking more about them.

So, ironically, the pressure to resist instant gratification can sometimes lead individuals into a trap of distraction. The more they try to avoid or suppress their desires, the more they find themselves fixated on the very temptations they are trying to resist. This constant battle against their natural inclinations can create a cycle of guilt, shame, and continuous failure.

When individuals fail to adhere to the ideals of delayed gratification, they often fall into a pattern of acute guilt and self-flagellation. They berate themselves for their perceived lack of willpower and discipline, which further damages their self-esteem and hinders their overall well-being.

Mark Thompson was a professional, striving for career advancement. Mark knew that investing time in continuous learning and skill development was crucial for his success. However, he found it challenging to resist some leisure activities such as binge-watching television series or spending time scrolling through social media. Each time he succumbed to these distractions, he experienced intense guilt and regret. He berated himself for his apparent lack of discipline and saw himself as unworthy of achieving his professional goals.

It is important to acknowledge that instant gratification is a natural human inclination and resisting it at all costs may not always be the healthiest approach. Instead of perpetuating a cycle of self-judgment and guilt, it is essential to adopt a balanced perspective. This involves understanding and accepting one's natural tendencies while finding ways to manage and navigate them effectively.

HOW TO STRIKE A BALANCE?

Let us explore the importance of embracing self-compassion and finding a middle ground between instant and delayed gratification. By understanding the nuanced relationship between our desires, goals, and well-being, we can foster a healthier and more sustainable approach to personal growth and fulfillment.

Understanding the Nuanced Relationship

To navigate the complexities of gratification, we must recognize the nuanced relationship between our desires, goals, and overall well-being. Instant gratification, when pursued without any consideration, can lead to impulsive choices and short-term pleasures that may hinder long-term progress. On the other hand, rigidly adhering to delayed gratification can create unnecessary stress, deprivation, and feelings of inadequacy. The key lies in striking a balance that aligns with our values and supports our personal growth journey.

Embracing Self-Compassion

In the pursuit of success and personal growth, finding a balance between instant and delayed gratification is essential.

Self-compassion serves as a powerful antidote to the self-judgment and guilt that often accompany our struggles with gratification. Rather than berating ourselves for giving in to temptations or feeling unworthy, we can cultivate self-compassion by offering kindness, understanding, and forgiveness to ourselves. This gentle approach acknowledges our humanity and recognizes that setbacks and challenges are a natural part of the growth process.

Sarah is a driven professional who strives for success in her career. Sarah has been following a strict regimen of delayed gratification, sacrificing personal time and leisure activities to achieve her goals. However, she often finds herself exhausted, burnt out, and lacking joy in her pursuits. By embracing self-compassion, Sarah learns to listen to her needs, set realistic boundaries, and incorporate moments of enjoyment and relaxation into her schedule. This shift allows her to maintain her drive while nurturing her well-being, ultimately leading to a more sustainable and fulfilling path to success.

Cultivating Mindful Awareness

Mindfulness plays a pivotal role in navigating the middle ground between instant and delayed gratification. By practicing mindful awareness, we develop the ability to observe our desires and impulses without immediate judgment or reaction. This awareness empowers us to make conscious choices that honor both our present well-being and long-term aspirations.

Finding the middle ground

Finding the middle ground between instant and delayed gratification involves integrating elements of both into our lives in a harmonious way. It requires us to identify our core values, align our actions with those values, and set realistic expectations for ourselves. By embracing a balanced approach, we can enjoy the present moment while working towards our long-term goals.

LET'S BREAK THE MYTH!

Stop judging yourself. Giving in to temptations doesn't make you bad. It doesn't imply that you're weak. You don't need to do things as per societal standards or as per the expectations of others. You do not need to live your life on external validation.

Focus on what seems important to you. Dive into your inner self and ask questions to determine your own goals and priorities. Then consider how you can reach them with self-compassion and acceptance.

Do not feel ashamed of your love for temptations. If you love food, accept it. I have a sweet tooth and I do not hesitate to say that. Do not deprive yourself completely of the things you love. Be empathetic towards yourselves. Respect your desires. If your mind finds something comforting or soothing, do not deprive it of that comfort. If you do so, your mind will feel starved and crave for those comforts. This can lead to anger and irritable behavior.

In times you are unable to resist temptations, do not be harsh with yourself. Do not curse or blame yourself for not being strong. Treat yourself with empathy and kindness. Soothe yourself with positive thoughts. Instead of backlashing yourself, console yourself for having done good, and inspire yourself to do better.

SAY OUT LOUD:

1. "I release the belief that suppressing my emotions is a necessary sacrifice for success, understanding that acknowledging and processing my feelings is integral to my well-being."

2. "I honor my desires and emotions as valuable guides on my journey, recognizing that they offer insights that contribute to a more fulfilling life."
3. "I embrace the ebb and flow of emotions, understanding that they are a natural part of the human experience, even in the pursuit of success."
4. "I release the need for strict control over every aspect of my life, acknowledging that flexibility and adaptability contribute to a more holistic sense of well-being."
5. "I embrace a compassionate mindset, releasing self-blame and judgment when faced with challenges in upholding my willpower."
6. "I understand that kindness and self-understanding can pave the way for resilience and positive change."

Chapter 7

The Vain Attempt of "Removing Temptations"

"On temptation – here is one of the most helpful guiding principles: it is easier to avoid temptation than it is to resist temptation."

- Lynn G. Robbins

"The best way to resist temptation is to avoid it. Prevention is far, far better than repentance."

- Spencer W. Kimball

Temptations are awfully tempting. They lure you, seduce you, and draw you towards themselves. The more you try to resist them, the more you are drawn towards them.

The self-improvement industry often advocates for the removal of distractions and temptations from our lives. We are made to believe that by eliminating external influences that divert our attention, we can cultivate unwavering focus and achieve our goals. However, the reality is that this technique is often short-lived, and leads to frustration, self-judgment, and a diminished sense of self-discipline.

Avoiding temptations, in other words, imagining they don't exist, is actually not the best way to resist them. Just considering that they do not matter to you, or thinking that they don't exist, cannot deny the fact that they are present, and you cannot completely do away with them. So, a person who spends a lot of time thinking about women, can fire female staff from the office, stop attending social gatherings, and avoid meeting female friends and colleagues, but that won't mean women would cease to exist on earth.

When you try to avoid temptations, you always know they are there. However much you keep removing them, trying not to come face to face with them, you will someday have to confront them. The vain attempt to remove temptations does not work for long.

I went on a diet a few months ago. I made sure I had only healthy food in my kitchen. I avoided cakes, sweets, candies, and chocolates at all costs. I thought I would never look at unhealthy stuff again. A week later my friends came over with a large chocolate cake. Everyone had sizable portions of it. I saw them relishing it, and enjoying it, while I looked at it and felt depressed. After refusing it half-heartedly, a few times, I finally agreed to have a bite, then another, another, and stopped only when we had finished it.

Resisting temptations only causes us to give in to them completely, resulting in a disaster. Oscar Wilde says, "The only way to get rid of a temptation is to yield to it. Resist it, and your soul grows sick with longing for the things it has forbidden to itself, with desire for what its monstrous laws have made monstrous and unlawful."

We live in a world inundated with distractions. It is practically impossible to eliminate things we love and crave for, in the desire to achieve remarkable feats. All things that we love and long for are available to us at the click of a button. They constantly vie for our attention, and it becomes greatly difficult to avoid them and resist them all the time.

When someone is unable to hold on to their desires and succumb to them, they are bound to feel like a failure and fall into a pit of self-doubt and self-criticism. By trying to remove temptations they set themselves up for disappointment and self-blame when they inevitably fall short.

In truth, discipline is not solely reliant on external circumstances. It is a deeply internal process that requires self-awareness, self-compassion, and an understanding of our unique strengths and limitations. Simply removing distractions does not guarantee discipline; it merely creates an illusion of control. True self-discipline comes from cultivating a strong sense of purpose, self-empathy, and understanding, and developing effective strategies to navigate distractions rather than attempting to eradicate them entirely.

Often people these days are distracted by social media. Our smartphones, and their endless notifications, do not let us concentrate on our work, and we end up checking our phones every now and then. We are often advised in this regard about turning off notifications, decluttering our physical spaces, and creating rigid schedules to minimize potential distractions. While these techniques may work for some time, they do not give the same results eventually because life is inherently filled with unexpected disruptions and temptations.

Trying to resist them will cause them to haunt you even more. It has also been seen that people who concentrate too much on creating a distraction-free environment, end up becoming hyperaware of every minor distraction. They start to look at the minutest things as distractions, and this spoils their peace of mind. Such people are also not likely to interact well with friends and colleagues, as they build a so-called protective shell around themselves within which they find their so-called distraction-free world. As a result, their family and social life suffer. This leads to frustration because of unhealthy relationships.

LET'S BREAK THIS MYTH!

We have often been misguided about removing temptations to create a distraction-free environment that guarantees success. The truth is that we need to focus on building a healthier relationship with distractions. We need to understand that we are humans. We need to respect our needs and desires and treat ourselves with empathy and understanding, instead of harshly denying ourselves everything we love.

Secondly, we need to understand that it's normal to sometimes fall short, it's okay to sometimes give in. We need not judge ourselves for it. We should not blame or curse ourselves for an occasional lapse in concentration.

Moreover, it is important to build internal resilience and accept occasional distractions as opportunities for growth and self-compassion. Instead of making futile attempts to eradicate distractions, we should try to embrace them as a part of the human experience.

1. "I acknowledge that true success comes from building the strength to navigate temptations, rather than attempting to eliminate them entirely."

2. "I choose to confront temptations as opportunities for self-discipline and personal growth, understanding that avoidance only postpones the challenge."

3. "I recognize that the illusion of control created by avoiding temptations is fleeting, and I focus on building a sustainable foundation of self-discipline."

4. "I empower myself to make conscious choices in the face of temptations, knowing that each decision contributes to my growth and success."

5. "I do not label myself as a sinner or a loser when I give in to temptations. Instead, I embrace my humanity, learning and growing from each experience with kindness and understanding."

6. "I recognize that succumbing to temptations sometimes doesn't define my worth; I choose compassion over self-condemnation, understanding that I am human and imperfect."

Chapter 8

The Blinding Focus on "End Result"

"I look into the future because that's where I'm going to spend the rest of my life."

- George Burns

"Focus on long-term success but be willing to make short adjustments to get there."

- Simon Sinek

In the goal-oriented society that prevails today, success gurus often swear by being futuristic, keeping your eyes on your future, and your focus on your goals. They say it helps you achieve the desired success.

While ambition and foresight are undoubtedly valuable traits, the constant focus on the future can overshadow the joy of living in the present moment. The perpetual wait for a brighter future can lead to a chronic state of dissatisfaction with the current circumstances, as happiness becomes a destination perpetually on the horizon. We tend to overlook the simple pleasures of life, the small victories, and the moments of genuine joy.

Eckhart Tolle, in his seminal work "The Power of Now," emphasizes the importance of being fully present and the detrimental consequences of focusing solely on your future goals. He asserts that the present moment is all we have, and by constantly looking toward the future, we forfeit the richness of life unfolding in the now. "Make the Now the primary focus of your life," he says.

When you constantly anticipate the future, you create a paradox. In the words of Tolle, "Stress is caused by being 'here' but wanting to be 'there' or being in the present but desiring the future." This results in overwhelm, anxiety, and unwanted stress.

Moreover, when we constantly focus on end results, we start to believe that happiness lies in a distant accomplishment and unknowingly create a mindset that does not realize the joy present in each unfolding moment. Living in the present moment is the gateway to mental peace. Too much preoccupation with future pursuits hampers your peace of mind. As Tolle suggests, "Don't let the mad world tell you that success is anything other than a successful present moment." True happiness is not a destination, but a journey; if we keep our eyes on our destination and overlook the beauties of the roads we traveled, the paths we trailed, and the bridges we crossed, we are missing out on all experiences, and learning that life has to offer.

Also, by consistently looking toward the future, individuals may foster a mindset that always focuses on what they lack rather than appreciating the abundance of the present. Living in the present is intricately linked with the practice of gratitude.

Gratitude, according to Buddha, is not merely a response to favorable circumstances but a way of life. "Let us rise up and be thankful, for if we didn't learn a lot today, at least we learned a little, and if we didn't learn a little, at least we didn't get sick, and if we got sick, at least we didn't die; so, let us all be thankful." This verse from "The Buddha's Guide to Gratitude" underscores the idea that whatever we have in the present, whether in the form of blessings, or challenges, there is always something to be grateful for.

Constantly waiting for life to improve can blind individuals to the richness of the present. True fulfillment arises not from an incessant focus on what is to come but from an appreciation of what is here and now.

Life always keeps offering unexpected challenges, and distractions. It's always not possible to maintain your focus consistently. Life is not always as you idealize. There may be tough times when you're unable to keep your focus on your goals. You may get sick. You may get an injury. There may be a hurricane or flooding. A friend or family may fall into trouble and need your assistance. Or you may have a tough work week and be completely exhausted. When individuals fail to meet their self-imposed expectations to maintain their constant gaze towards the horizon, they may label themselves as unambitious, and end up in self-doubt. In such times it is important to understand your priorities in life and create a balance between your goals and your present circumstances.

A relentless pursuit of a brighter future often ensnares people in a cycle of anxiety and impatience. The paradoxical nature of perpetual anticipation prevents the cultivation of gratitude and mindfulness.

Mindfulness is an essential aspect of living in the present. It helps you to reflect on your past, find peace in the present, and create a positive vision for the future.

A healthy and positive vision of the future can only be achieved if we savor the beauty of the present. Only when we create a beautiful now, can we dream of a beautiful future because the future is nowhere, you will never enter the future. You can only live in a now. So, the prime focus of our life should be on relishing and appreciating our present.

The results of your endeavor can only provide you with momentary motivation. Real motivation only comes when you savor the journey, you enjoy the process. Only then your motivation stays there forever.

I recall a very funny incident, that my close friend told me about. I would like to share it with you so that you understand the importance of enjoying your journey, on a lighter note.

My friend didn't like to get up early in the morning to go to the gym (like most of us). I mean, he wanted to get fit. I remember his hostel room was always adorned with posters of celebs with great abs and muscular bodies. But he hated going to the gym.

He often switched off the alarm when it rang in the morning and forgot about it. Then after two days of consecutively missing the gym, he was loaded with tons of guilt. The next day he would promptly get up and hit the gym. He would feel energetic and highly motivated and decide he would never miss the gym again.

The next day he would charge off towards the gym at the first ring of the alarm. This would continue for the next few days (energy going down a bit). By the end of the week, he would be somehow dragging himself out of bed. The next day he would say to himself that he's probably not feeling well and switch off the alarm. He would miss the gym two days in a row.

He would develop guilt again. He would curse himself, beat himself, and kick himself to the gym.

This day he reaches the gym to find a beautiful young woman who is a new entry to the gym. They exchange glances. They smile at each other. She approaches him for assistance and expert advice. His heartbeat rises.

He never needed an alarm again!

PS: Find an attractive partner if you never want to miss your gym routine.

The moral of the story is that the end results can only give you momentary motivation. You will do things, and do them forever, and do them even better only when you love doing them.

When you love the journey, your journey is motivation enough to take you to your goals. So, we should focus on making a beautiful and happy present rather than awaiting happiness in the future.

Success should not be viewed solely through the lens of future accomplishments but rather as a holistic journey that encompasses the present. By finding a balance between future aspirations and present appreciation, individuals can unlock a richer, and more meaningful life.

SAY OUT LOUD:

1. "I am worthy of joy in the present moment, regardless of my future goals."
2. "I embrace the beauty of now, finding happiness in the little moments of life."
3. "My self-worth is not determined solely by my ability to focus on my goals."
4. I release the need to constantly wait for a better tomorrow and appreciate the present."
5. "Success is a journey, and I am allowed to relish each step along the way."
6. "I celebrate my achievements in the now and do not wait for an unforeseen future."
7. "My worth is not diminished by uncertainty or lack of clear goals."
8. "Each day is an opportunity to enjoy the journey, and I allow myself to relish it."
9. "I honor the process of growth and understand that it takes time to achieve goals."
10. "I am not alone in feeling the struggle between the present and the future; it's a shared human experience."

Chapter 9

The Relentless "Pursuit of Success"

"If you reach your goal: set a bigger goal. If you get to the top of a mountain: find a bigger mountain!"

- Unknown

"The man who can drive himself further once the effort gets painful is the man who will win."

- Sir Roger Bannister

Today, there is this universal belief that success can bring us profound happiness. Actually, we are not wrong. Success does bring us happiness if the meaning of success is not limited to professional achievements and material gains. If success is taken for its intrinsic value of inner growth, and personal well-being, then indeed it is indispensable for our true happiness and fulfillment in life.

The problem lies in the fact that 'the success', which the whole world is running behind, is a mere quest for more and more wealth, power, fame, and recognition. We are often advised to work hard, build self-discipline, stay committed, and climb the ladder to achieve our goals. We are brainwashed with countless success stories, each telling us about pushing our limits, taking the pain, utilizing every second of our day, and believing in ourselves. We are told by society that achieving this so-called success is the sole aim of our lives. And we all begin to believe this. We create the success mindset.

But there comes a point when our ambition morphs into obsession; transforming us into inadvertent workaholics; when the quest for success becomes an intense craving, and when it takes the form of an unquenchable thirst for achievements.

In the pursuit of success, it can often become tough to know where to draw the line. When individuals become overly ambitious, they may find themselves trapped in a constant cycle of striving for more. They always feel unsatisfied even after they have achieved their desired level of success.

This relentless pursuit of success has a very dark side to it. Too much ambition often leads to unhappiness; let's see how:

1.   Impact on mental health

People who make success the sole aim of their lives often end up neglecting their health and wellness. Long working hours, and demanding work schedules lead to tiredness and fatigue. On top of that, work stress, deadlines, competition, and constant pressure to achieve set goals lead to anxiety, stress, and frustration. The obsession with work and success reaches its limit until the wake-up call comes in the form of burnout.

Often people look at their achievements as a marker of their self-worth. In such a case, they constantly fear failure and this fear takes a toll on their mental health. Moreover, any challenges or setbacks set them reeling into a whirlwind of inadequacy and low self-esteem. They internalize failures as shortcomings and end up in self-criticism and self-doubt.

Success can also sometimes make you feel isolated. When a person achieves high levels of success, it can get difficult to find people who can relate to them or the experiences or struggles that they have been through. They may always have to seem in control and put on a brave face even when they are struggling inside. This causes them to feel lonely and isolated. They may feel that they have none to share their true feelings with. This is often the case with highly successful people who end up in depression. Their outer life seems so desirable to the world when they are in hell inside.

2. Impact on relationships

A person driven by excessive ambition may have trouble with empathy and emotional intelligence. Their single-minded focus on success can make it difficult for them to truly connect with others and understand their needs and emotions. Moreover, the pursuit of success often requires significant time and energy, leaving little room for nurturing meaningful connections with others, as a result of which friendships, romantic relationships, and even family bonds can suffer.

Relationships require time and effort. Our loved ones need much more than the material gifts we can bestow upon them. They need our love and care. When people adhere too much importance to their careers or achievements, they often neglect their friends and family, which results in stressed relationships.

3. Impact on mindset

Often people measure their success through the lens of comparison. When accomplishments are weighed against others, and self-worth is contingent on outshining peers, it leads to perpetual dissatisfaction. Our minds become the breeding ground for an insatiable appetite for more. "Comparison is the thief of joy," warns Theodore Roosevelt.

Another cost of success is the unwanted pressure to continually perform at a high level. Once an individual attains a certain level of success, there is often the pressure to constantly outperform oneself to meet the expectations of the onlookers. This can be extremely overwhelming and exhausting.

Moreover, this incessant drive for success can lead individuals to compromise their values, forsake their passions, and barter their authenticity for societal approval. Aren't we seeing how the present generation yearns to become successful? They want it at any cost and are ready to do anything it takes (good or bad) to attain their goals. This success mindset is coercing people into pursuing success at the expense of their values, beliefs, and passions.

4. Impact on our true happiness

"Success is getting what you want; happiness is wanting what you get," says Dale Carnegie. While success is all about wanting more, it often becomes an unquenchable thirst. On the other hand, happiness is all about accepting and appreciating what we have. Yet, this distinction is often blurred in the relentless pursuit of success. "Success is not the key to happiness. Happiness is the key to success. If you love what you are doing, you will be successful." says Albert Schweitzer.

In running behind success, often people miss the moments of true joy in life. They fail to observe happiness in everyday situations like spending time with yourself, or in nature, laughing with your family, caring for others, or getting spiritually connected. In awaiting the bigger happiness in life, they miss out on the small instances of life that are the reminders of a truly joyous life. The little joys of everyday life make memories that you actually cherish lifelong. These are the memories that when you look back, remind you how fortunate you are. These wonderful moments help you develop gratefulness towards life.

LET'S BREAK THIS MYTH!

Andrew Wilkinson, founder of Meta Lab says, "You don't have to make yourself miserable to be successful."

Being productive and successful doesn't have to come at the cost of your happiness. Success is not the only thing that matters in life. It is important to find a balance between success and other aspects of life that bring us joy and fulfillment such as family, friends, hobbies, and personal growth.

Before we run behind the so-called success, we first need to examine our motives. This is important in order to help us differentiate between healthy ambition and obsession. If our purpose is personal development, inner fulfillment, or the betterment of a loved one, then our pursuit of success may be understood. But if your sole purpose is seeking validation, competition, comparison, or satisfying your ego, then you might re-evaluate your priorities.

Stop taking life as a race. When you live a life competing and comparing yourself with others, you weigh your self-worth against other's achievements, and that's the wrong thing to do. You need to understand that everyone's journey is unique, and everyone's purpose and priorities in life are different.

A better way of thinking can be comparing yourself to yourself. This will help you see how far you've come and will help you appreciate your progress.

You need to define your own version of success and reflect on what truly matters to you. Then set goals that align with your personal definition of success.

Prioritizing self-care is another important aspect of a balanced life. Making time for activities that enhance your physical, mental, and spiritual well-being is vital for a healthy lifestyle. It is also equally important to hear and understand your emotions. Treat yourself with empathy and kindness, because if you won't, who will?

Invest your time in cultivating healthy relationships. I always say, "Relationships need time and effort". When relationships are left uncared for, they become dry. I heard a song back in my school days, "Love that is kept inside, will surely fade someday."

We need to give quality time to our love and family relations. Romantic moments with our partner, playtime with kids and pets, a fun time with family, and an evening with friends, are all equally important tasks that need to be prioritized on your to-do list on a regular basis. The joy of happy relationships is the marker of a truly successful and fulfilling life.

Another great aspect of a truly successful life should be cultivating gratitude. Your success will feel like no success to you if you do not know how to appreciate and celebrate what you have. Only when you learn to count your blessings you can shift your focus from what you want, to what you have. Accepting and appreciating everything that life brings to you is the real way of living a happy and contented life.

So, take a step back, define what success means to you by reassessing your priorities, and find a balance between ambition and personal well-being, to achieve a sustainable and fulfilling success.

SAY OUT LOUD!

1. "My worth is not solely determined by my accomplishments; I am inherently valuable regardless of external measures."
2. "I release the need for comparison, understanding that my journey is unique and unfolds at its own perfect pace."
3. "My ambitions are tempered with self-awareness, ensuring I pursue success without sacrificing my well-being."
4. "I honor the importance of rest, rejuvenation, and maintaining a healthy work-life balance on my path to success."

5. "My daily routine includes moments of self-reflection, meditation, and gratitude, enhancing my mental well-being and overall happiness."
6. "I express gratitude daily, acknowledging the positive aspects of my life, fostering a mindset of abundance and contentment."
7. "I cherish and prioritize family time, creating memories that contribute to the richness of my life."
8. "I understand that meaningful relationships require time and effort; I invest in the well-being of my friends and family with genuine care."
9. "I prioritize family dinners and gatherings, creating opportunities for meaningful conversation and shared laughter."
10. "My success is a reflection of my holistic well-being; I prioritize mental and emotional health as essential components of a prosperous life."

To Be Yourself

"To be yourself in a world that is constantly trying to make you something else is the greatest accomplishment."

- Ralph Waldo Emerson

The world is teeming with influences- from societal norms to media portrayals. In this world, the journey to be oneself is fraught with challenges. The external clamor, and the incessant desire to conform to set standards, drown the inner voice, compelling individuals to mold themselves into shapes society deems acceptable.

We are all trying to be someone else. We are not ready to accept ourselves for what we are but are most of the time trying to live a life that is not ours, chase dreams that do not belong to us, and even develop a personality that does not resonate with us. Why can't we just love who we are, accept and appreciate what we have, and savor the life we live?

It requires a great deal of courage. Courage to battle societal expectations, and courage to stand firm in one's authenticity. But before we portray to the world our unique self, we need self-discovery. We need to understand and willfully accept ourselves, our abilities, and our uniqueness. We need to shift our focus from societal expectations and standards and embrace authenticity.

Embracing Authenticity

Authenticity demands a deep exploration of our values, passions, and beliefs. It demands not only discovering our identity but also placing trust in it. It requires us to say to ourselves, "I am what I am, and I am enough." We need to acknowledge the uniqueness that resides within us and celebrate our individuality.

The greatest accomplishment lies not only in discovering ourselves but also in having the courage to present ourselves to the world. It is important to rise above the fear of judgment, or rejection, and present to the world your authentic self.

Embracing our true self is not a destination but a continuous journey. It involves a commitment to self-growth, a willingness to evolve, and an acceptance of the ever-changing nature of identity. It is an ongoing process of becoming attuned to our authentic essence.

By being true to ourselves, we not only liberate our own spirits but also inspire others to embark on their journeys of self-discovery. It serves as a beacon of light that empowers others to accept and embrace their identity.

When each of us learns to embrace authenticity, we can help relieve the world of the burden of expectations, judgment, and conformity. We can create a world in which every being loves to be. We can build a genuine world, with genuine people.

I hope this book helps its readers take a second thought upon their embedded beliefs and helps them take their first step toward self-realization. Little courageous steps from individuals like you and me can help create a world free from judgment, and expectations; a world where everyone lives their life the way they want to; where everyone lives for themselves, not to please others; where everyone can show the world their real self; a world where everyone loves themselves for what they are.

No More Hating Yourself

The famous American author and speaker Shawn Achor says, "As we got more interested in time management and productivity, we lost the individual, and with that loss, we lost happiness as well. So, I think the world has actually been malnourished as we've focused so much on productivity and ignored happiness and meaning to our own detriment."

Do not make self-improvement the focus of all your endeavors. When you are looking only for improvement, you are loading yourself with a ton of limiting beliefs. When you are bombarded with concepts like building self-discipline, willpower, and determination, you start looking for them all around you. When you don't find them, you panic. You feel a perceived lack and begin to improve yourself, inculcating within yourself values and beliefs you do not resonate with. You completely ignore and undermine your hidden virtues.

You forget the person you are. And you lose yourself in your quest for self-improvement.

It's like a cub that grew up amongst a herd of sheep and was made to believe that it was a disabled sheep. It kept trying to be like them, it tried to bleat. It was ridiculed by its peers, and instructed by the others to try to follow others and see and do what others did. So, it did. It kept trying to improve. It never looked at how different it was and remained completely ignorant of its power and might. It remained subject to rejection and ridicule from its peers when what it actually deserved was their awe, admiration, and respect. What a pity it was that a glorious being never realized its glory and remained battling its uniqueness to conform to the accepted standards.

Do not accept your unique abilities as your disabilities. The world will try to compare you with their so-called normal. They will try to mold and shape you in their preset cookie-cutter molds. They will tell you that you need to improve. But it's time you say, NO!

Say NO to improving yourself. Say NO to hating yourself.

Can I Ask You a Favor?

If "9 Ways to Hate Yourself", helped change your perspective of self-improvement; if it made you think about discovering and accepting the real you; if it made you a little more confident about yourself; **don't forget to leave a review on Amazon**. It would really mean a lot to me!

If you liked my work, please follow me on my Amazon Author Page. Your support means a lot to an upcoming author like me.

You can also follow me on Bookbub where my books are often available at huge discounts. Also, you'll be notified about my latest releases so that you can grab them at their launch price.

Also, if you haven't downloaded your free book "Thoughts for Your Soul", you can   get it here!

My Books

I have been writing for a while now. It has been an amazing journey of learning and sharing my experiences with my readers. If you haven't read any of my previous books, here's the list. All these books are available on Amazon. I hope you like them as you liked "9 Ways to Hate Yourself".

The Perfect Book for Imperfect Couples – The Most Powerful Approach to Build a Happy Relationship for Life.

The Perfect Workbook – Because Relationships Need a Little Effort.

Heal Your Conflicts – A Couple's Bible for Managing Conflicts, Healing Emotional Wounds, Saving Your Marriage, and Building Lasting Happiness.

7 Great Habits of Success – Discover the power of Habits for Self-Improvement, Build Internal Motivation, Create Growth Mindset, and Crack the Secret Code of Highly Successful People.

* 9 7 9 8 8 7 6 7 4 4 1 7 3 *